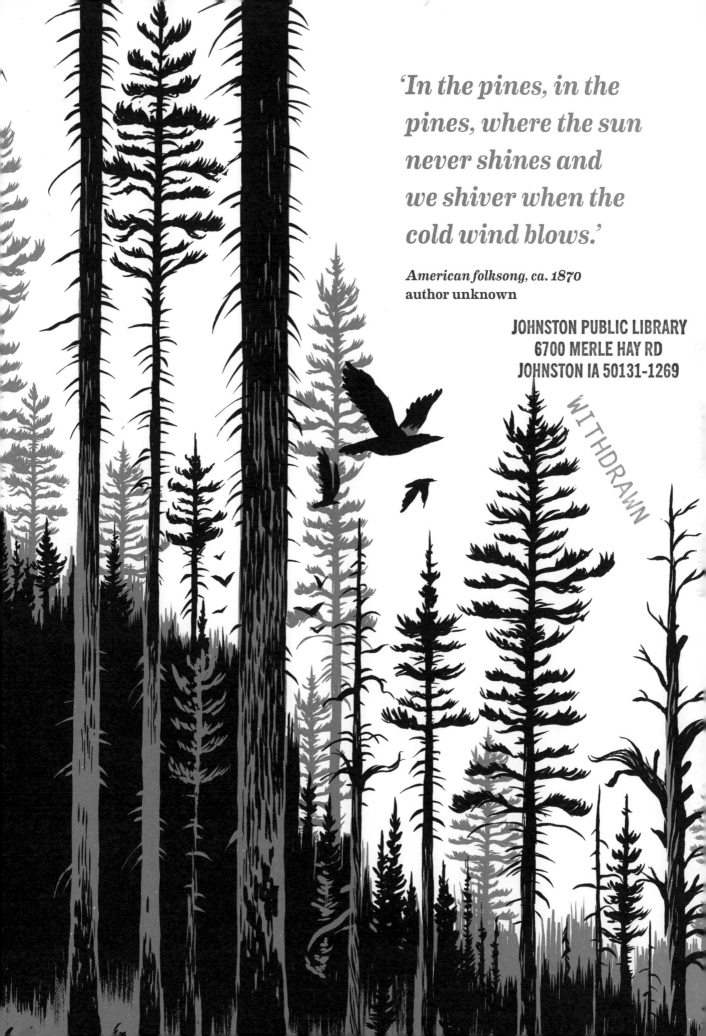

'In the pines, in the pines, where the sun never shines and we shiver when the cold wind blows.'

American folksong, ca. 1870
author unknown

CONTENTS

PRETTY POLLY
and the
SHIP'S CARPENTER

I'LL TAKE THE HELM, GET YOURSELF BELOW AND INTO SOME DRY CLOTHES!

AYE, AYE!

ANOTHER ONE?

HOW MANY HAVE WE LOST SO FAR?

THREE, SIR, SINCE THE STORM BEGAN.

WELL, MR. BRIGGS, WE WON'T HAVE A CREW LEFT IF THIS GALE PERSISTS.

MAYBE IF WE STEER SOUTH IT WOULD...

OUT OF THE QUESTION! WE'VE ALL SEEN BAD WEATHER BEFORE.

HAVE SOME HANDS RIG EXTRA SAFETY LINES AND MAN THE PUMPS. THE REST STAY BELOW.

AYE SIR!

POLLY? LISTEN...

BEFORE WE GET MARRIED I WOULD LIKE...

MARRIED? WE CAN'T GET MARRIED! MY FATHER WOULD *NEVER* ALLOW IT. I THOUGHT WE DISCUSSED THIS.

... I KNOW... I APOLOGIZE. I MEAN... GOD, HOW I *LOVE* YOU!

I KNOW, STUPID BOY! WHY CAN'T WE JUST ENJOY THAT LOVE, HERE AND NOW?

I'VE PREPARED A SURPRISE FOR YOU.

A SURPRISE? FOR ME? HOW SWEET!

WHERE IS IT?

NOT FAR. COME AND I'LL SHOW YOU.

WHO, ME? I'M THE KIND OF GIRL THAT STAYS TRUE, WILL CLAYTON!

SO YOU DENY IT, THEN? YOU DENY YOU WERE SEEN AROUND TOWN WITH OTHER MEN?

WELL, AN ELIGIBLE YOUNG LADY LIKE MYSELF HAS MANY SUITORS, DON'T YOU KNOW? SOME ARE VERY *HANDSOME* AND VERY *RICH*, UNLIKE OTHERS!

DO *NOT* MOCK ME!

WHAT HAPPENED? DID YOU BREAK UP WITH HER?

OH MY DEAR, DEAR BOY! I KNOW IT HURTS! SURE I DO, BUT I TOLD YOU TIME AND AGAIN: YOU'RE TOO GOOD FOR HER. SHE'S NOTHING BUT A SPOILED LITTLE *WHORE!*

DON'T YOU CALL HER THAT, MOTHER!

I'M SORRY, WILLIE, BUT SHE WAS SEEN GALLIVANTING AROUND TOWN, FLIRTING WITH ALL KINDS OF MEN.

WHERE ARE YOU GOING? SUPPER WILL BE READY SOON.

GOT SOMETHING I HAVE TO DO. DON'T WAIT UP FOR ME.

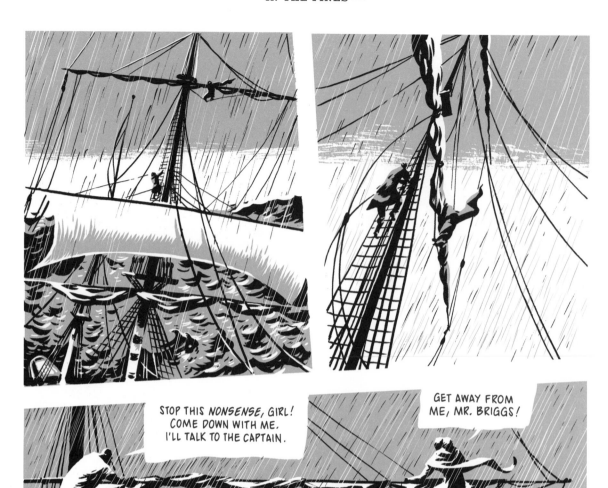

STOP THIS *NONSENSE, GIRL!* COME DOWN WITH ME. I'LL TALK TO THE CAPTAIN.

GET AWAY FROM ME, MR. BRIGGS!

COME! GRAB MY HAND!

SHE WON'T LET ME! DON'T YOU SEE?

I *KILLED* HER!

WILLIE?
IS THAT YOU?

OH MY, BUT YOU
LOOK A FRIGHT!
WHERE ON EARTH
HAVE YOU BEEN?

NEVER
YOU MIND,
MOTHER.
I'VE COME TO
SAY GOODBYE.
I'LL BE GOING
AWAY FOR
A WHILE.

PLEASE DON'T
CRY, MOTHER.
NOT FOR ME.

I THOUGHT I COULD GET FREE OF HER BUT SHE FOLLOWED ME TO SEA!

I'LL MAKE AN END OF IT. IT'S ME SHE WANTS...

NO!

THE LONG BLACK VEIL

LOOK, SON, I'VE GOT SEVEN WITNESSES THAT HAVE TESTIFIED THEY SAW YOU SHOOT AND KILL MR. PEABODY.

THEY LATER RECOGNIZED YOUR BLACK STETSON HAT AND THE COLT NAVY PISTOL FOUND ON YOUR PERSON THAT EVENING.

YOU CLAIM THAT YOU WERE SOMEWHERE ELSE WHEN THE KILLING TOOK PLACE. CAN YOU PRODUCE AN ALIBI?

NO, YOUR HONOR. AS I HAVE STATED BEFORE, I WAS JUST OUT FOR A STROLL.

I WISH I COULD HAVE DONE MORE TO HELP HIM.

IN THE END HE ALMOST SEEMED RESIGNED TO HIS FATE.

WHO COULD HAVE THOUGHT THAT *DANIEL,* OF ALL PEOPLE, COULD BE CAPABLE OF SUCH A TERRIBLE DEED?

I GUESS YOU NEVER *REALLY* GET TO KNOW FOLKS. NOT EVEN THE ONES THAT ARE CLOSEST TO YOU.

WHERE WERE YOU? I EXPECTED YOU HOME HOURS AGO!

...SORRY, MY DARLIN'... I DIDN'T WANT TO WAKE YOU...

TANEYTOWN

HA HA HA! NO, DON'T...
YOU NAUGHTY MAN!
OOH... OH... MH...

THAT SURE IS A MIGHTY BIG KNIFE YOU GOT THERE, SON.

I AIN'T YOUR SON.

MY DADDY GAVE ME THIS HERE KNIFE, KILLED HIM SOME KRAUTS WITH IT, TOO, OVER IN FRANCE, HE DID.

MY DADDY IS A BIG *WAR HERO*, FIGHTING IN THE TRENCHES WITH THE 396th.

SMACK!

YOUR DADDY AIN'T NOTHIN' BUT A WASHED OUT *DRUNK!* YOU HEAR ME, CALBERT BROWN?

WHAT AM I GOING TO DO WITH HIM? HE'S NEARLY A GROWN MAN, BUT HE'S SLOW IN THE HEAD!

DON'T MIND HIM. TONIGHT I'LL TAKE YOU TO THAT NEW JOINT IN GETTYSBURG. IT'LL BE JUST YOU AND ME.

THAT'S A FINE PIECE OF STEEL! AIN'T NO STANDARD ISSUE, NEITHER.

NO, INDEED! MY GRANDDADDY GAVE ME THIS KNIFE. KILLED HIM SOME REBS WITH IT IN '63.

NICE.

FIGURED IT'D KILL SOME KRAUTS JUST AS WELL.

AND IF I DO MAKE IT HOME OUT OF THIS HELL SOMEDAY, I'LL PASS THIS KNIFE ON TO MY OWN SON. HE MUST BE ALMOST TWELVE NOW. HAVEN'T SEEN HIM SINCE I ENLISTED...

AND WHERE DO YOU LAY YOUR HAT, PRIVATE BROWN?

TANEYTOWN, MARYLAND. YOU WO...

BOOM

HEY, YOU! BOY! WHAT ARE YOU DOING HERE?

I... I AIN'T LOOKIN' FOR NO TROUBLE. I'M JUST LOOKING FOR MY DAD...

AIN'T NO COLOREDS IN THIS PART OF TOWN. NIGGERS ALL LIVE DOWN THAT WAY, 'CROSS THE TRACKS.

WHERE'D YOU SAY YOUR DADDY LIVES?

I DON'T KNOW, EXACTLY... JUST TANEYTOWN. I DON'T... ...SORRY... I...

OH, HI! YOU'RE EARLY.

MISS LILLY.

DID YOU HEAR ABOUT THAT BOY THEY HANGED OVER IN TANEYTOWN?

NO?

THEY CAUGHT THAT BOY STABBING SOME WHITE KID. THEY STRUNG HIM UP ON THE OLD TRESTLE BRIDGE, JUST LIKE THAT!

OH, MY? A LYNCHING?

GUESS SO! POOR BOY PLEADED FOR HIS LIFE. SAID HE JUST FOUND A BLOODIED KNIFE BY THE SIDE OF THE TRACKS.

DO YOU HEAR THAT, CALBERT BROWN? THAT'S HOW THEY TREAT US FOLKS OVER IN TANEYTOWN!

DON'T WORRY, MOMMA, I WON'T EVER GO THERE...

...ANYMORE.

MURDERER...

CALEB MEYER

NELLIE...

WHOA, YOU'RE UP EARLY! EVEN BY *YOUR* STANDARDS.

I'VE GOT A LOT OF CHORES TODAY...

AIN'T NOTHING BETTER FOR A HUNGRY MAN THAN A HOMEMADE LUNCH!

BUT ACTUALLY, I'D RATHER YOU DIDN'T STRAIN YOURSELF IN THIS HEAT.

I FEEL JUST FINE, JOHN!

I JUST WOULDN'T BE ABLE TO FORGIVE MYSELF IF WE WERE TO LOSE *ANOTHER BABY...*

I RECKON IT'S IN GOD'S HANDS.

I'D BETTER GET BACK TO WORK. THE DAY IS HALF DONE ALREADY AND TIME'S A-WASTING.

IT'S WITH CHORES LIKE THESE THAT I MISS CALEB MOST. MY LORD, BUT THAT FELLA COULD LIFT A TON WITHOUT SO MUCH AS BATTING AN EYE!

HNF...

WHAT'S THAT YOU SAID?

HM? NOTHING...

I'M HEADING BACK. I STILL HAVE A LOT OF WORK AT THE HOUSE, OK?

I CAN'T FIND ANY MEDICAL REASON WHY SHE MISCARRIED. SHE IS ONE VERY HEALTHY YOUNG WOMAN.

HOW MUCH DO I OWE YOU, DOC? I CAN'T PAY YOU NOW BUT PERHAPS AFTER THE HARVEST...

OH, NEVER-MIND JOHN, THAT'S QUITE ALRIGHT!

YOU JUST CONCERN YOURSELF WITH LOOKIN' AFTER NELLIE NOW, YOU HEAR?

SEE YOU IN CHURCH SUNDAY?

SURE THING! GOD BLESS YOU, DOC! YOU'RE A GOOD MAN, BE SEEING YOU ON SUNDAY THEN!

I'LL BE SEEING YOU, NELLIE...

DID SOME HARD WORKIN' TODAY. RECKON I CAN MOVE ON TO THE NORTH MEADOW SOON.

HARD TO FIND GOOD HIRED HELP. SINCE CALEB LEFT I HAVEN'T HAD ANYONE AS RELIABLE. WHY'D HE LEAVE? AND WITHOUT EVEN A WORD?

I DON'T KNOW...

MAYBE HE'S GONE WEST. THEY SAY YOU CAN MAKE A FORTUNE OVER THERE PICKING ORANGES.

YES, MAYBE. THERE'S NOTHING TO KEEP HIM HERE!

OOH!

WHAT'S WRONG?

NOTHING... I THINK I JUST FELT THE BABY MOVE... YES! THERE IT IS! COME AND FEEL!

YES! I FEEL IT! THANK THE LORD!

NELLIE KANE...

WHAT DID THE SHERIFF WANT?

HE TOLD ME THEY FOUND AN ILLEGAL STILL OVER AT CALEB'S PLACE. FOR MAKIN' *WHISKEY!*

SHERIFF SAYS HE MIGHT HAVE GOTTEN INTO TROUBLE WITH *BOOTLEGGERS* AND SUCH.

I HAD NO IDEA. HAD YOU?

HE WANTED TO KNOW WHEN WE LAST SAW CALEB. WELL, THAT MUST HAVE BEEN WELL OVER SIX MONTHS AGO, RIGHT?

HELPED ME OUT WITH THAT DARNED BARN ROOF, HE DID, REMEMBER?

YOU AIN'T SEEN HIM SINCE THEN EITHER, OR *HAVE* YOU?

ME? NO.

WELL, APPARENTLY HE'S STILL MISSING. SHERIFF'S COMBING THE ENTIRE COUNTY FOR HIM.

YOU COMIN' INSIDE?

I... I'LL ONLY BE A MINUTE...

DON'T BE UPSET, HONEY. HE'S BOUND TO TURN UP ONE OF THESE DAYS.

NO, HE AIN'T...

HELLO, NELLIE.

MR. MEYER! WHAT BRINGS *YOU* OUT IN THIS COLD?

NOTHING MUCH. JUST BEING NEIGHBOURLY I GUESS...

HEH HEH.

IS THAT *LIQUOR* YOU'RE DRINKING THERE, MR. MEYER?

HUSH! YOUR HUSBAND WILL HEAR! HEH, HEH!

WHERE'D YOU GET HOLD OF *THAT*?

MADE IT MYSELF. JUST SOMETHING TO PASS THE TIME.

WHY DON'T YOU GO AHEAD AND HAVE A TASTE? COME ON, LIVE A LITTLE!

NO, THANK YOU KINDLY, MR. MEYER. YOU GO ON NOW, HAVE A GOOD DAY...

MY NAME IS *CALEB!* PLEASE CALL ME *CALEB!*

AS YOU WISH.

NO THANK YOU, *CALEB!* NOW, GOOD DAY TO YOU!

YOUR HUSBAND. HE'S NOT HERE. WHERE IS HE?

JOHN HAS GONE TO BOWLING GREEN TO DO SOME BUSINESS THERE...,

DID HE GO DOWN THE MOUNTAINSIDE LEAVING YOU ALL ALONE? HEY! I'M TALKING TO YOU!

COME ON! JUST ONE LITTLE SIP!

PLEASE NO, CALEB! LET GO OF ME!

MUST'VE WASHED DOWN THIS GULLY WHEN THE SNOW MELTED.

BEEN LYING HERE FOR A GOODY TIME TOO, BY THE LOOK OF HIM.

WELL, HE PROBABLY FELL OFF A BLUFF FURTHER UP, BLIND DRUNK ON HIS OWN *HOOCH* NO DOUBT. POOR BASTARD.

BETTER CALL THE DOC. GET THE BOYS TO HELP HIM CLEAN UP THIS MESS...

ERROLL! HERE, BOY!

WHERE THE WILD ROSES GROW

SEE? TOLD YA! AIN'T NO CHAIN'S GONNA STOP ME!

FREE!

NOW, AS FOR THAT *OTHER* THING THAT WAS HOLDING ME BACK...

K RK

♪ ...WHEN I STRAYED WITH MY LOVE TO THE PURE CRYSTAL FOUNTAIN... ♪

♪ ...SHE WAS LOVELY AND FAIR AS THE ROSE OF SUMMER... ♪

THE DOGS HAVE DEFINITELY CAUGHT A WHIFF OF SOMETHING. HOW FAR DO YOU RECKON HE COULD HAVE GOT?

HE CAN'T BE MORE THAN A COUPLE OF HOURS AHEAD OF US. WE'RE CLOSING IN.

YOU KNOW, MY FATHER USED TO CALL ME WILD ROSE ALL THE TIME.

THE TRAIL LEADS TO THAT FARMHOUSE.

WAIT JUST ONE MINUTE!

THIS IS OLD JACK McDAY'S FARM! THAT'S HIS HOUSE OVER THERE.

JACK McDAY? YOU DON'T MEAN...

YES I DO! JACK McDAY AND HIS *WILD ROSE GANG!* INFAMOUS IN OVER SEVENTEEN COUNTIES! ROBBED A FAIR AMOUNT OF BANKS BEFORE THEY CAUGHT HIM.

NOW HE AND HIS GANG ARE DOING HARD TIME IN FEDERAL PRISON. WELL, MOST OF HIS GANG, ANYWAY. THEY NEVER GOT THE GIRL THAT THE GANG WAS NAMED AFTER. SHE WAS THE WORST OF THEM.

MORE THAN HALF THE MONEY HE STOLE WAS NEVER RECOVERED. ACCORDING TO JACK IT WAS ALL BURNED, BUT RUMOR HAS IT HE BURIED IT SOMEWHERE.

MURDER BALLADS

by Jan Donkers

Murder Ballads? But isn't that the title of a Nick Cave album? Sure it is, and the album is a gem in the genre, but the term stands for a lot more. Murder ballads were (and still are) an important element of the Great American Songbook — the unofficial anthology of popular music — and a sub-genre of the traditional ballad. The lyrics of these ballads all deal with a murder, but the way the story is told can differ considerably. Sometimes we follow that story from the point of view of the murderer, sometimes even from the point of view of the victim, but more often from the point of view of an observing third person — the narrator/singer. The development of the drama comes in different forms as well, but often the killer doesn't escape his (or her) fate and ends up at the gallows or behind bars, and the singer concludes with a moralistic argument: don't do it, 'cause you see where it will lead you! A fine depiction of 19th century America, where gun violence and religiously-inspired moralism tried to balance each other out. Yet, this is not a strictly American genre, because many of the ballads originated in England and were brought to the US by immigrants and adapted, passed down orally, and recycled in the form of a song to recount more or less gruesome incidents.

Erik Kriek has taken five of these ballads, recent as well as traditional, as starting points for his graphic stories, drawn in his characteristic suspenseful and nightmare-invoking style. But he has done much more than just adapt a song into a comic strip. Kriek has taken the lyrics as a starting point and delved into the history, as well as his own imagination, and taken the liberty to turn them into his own, broader pictorial stories — thereby giving us new, independent works of art.

The first story, PRETTY POLLY is a good example of that process. The song, with its multiple points of view, has been performed by a variety of artists, ranging from The Stanley Brothers to The Byrds, from Sandy Denny to Judy Collins. All of them have limited themselves to the simpler version of the song, which does not include the things the future has in store for Willie. He is not a murderer who arouses mixed feelings: the fact that he has already dug the grave for pregnant Polly before killing her makes him, according to Rennie Sparks (half of The Handsome Family, who have created memorable contributions to the genre themselves), a "creep," a "snickering psycho," and a present day serial killer comparable to Ted Bundy. For his interpretation of this ballad, Kriek has chosen the original, English version, which dates back to the first half of the 18th century and was known as "The Gosport Tragedy" or "The Cruel Ship's Carpenter." In this text, Willie is indeed a ship's carpenter who calls down a curse upon the ship on which he sails. It was common superstition at the time among British sailors that the ship was doomed if there was a murderer on board.

LONG BLACK VEIL, probably the best known of these five ballads, has a much shorter history and is not based upon just one historic event. The song was written by Marijohn Wilkin and Danny Dill in 1959 and was made into a country & western hit when Lefty Frizzell recorded his version. The songwriters combined three events into a tragic ballad about a man who, the noose already around his neck, refuses to reveal his alibi — protecting the honor of his lover is more important to him than his urge to survive. The unresolved murder of a priest was one of the events, and the mystery of the veiled woman, who visited, almost every day, the grave of movie star/heartbreaker Rudolph Valentino, gave the song its gloomy yet romantic coda. "Long Black Veil" is a song that is part of the standard repertoire of many an artist in the Americana genre but not only there. The version by The Band is the best known, but the song was also covered by Johnny Cash, Mick Jagger with The Chieftains, Nick Cave, The Grateful Dead, Chip Taylor, Jason and The Scorchers... The entire list would fill almost a whole page.

TARRYTOWN is not based upon a historic event but was invented by Steve Earle, who not only found inspiration for the song, but also for a short story of the same title in his book *Doghouse Roses*. First there was the song, he said later, but after finishing the story and giving his characters more flesh and blood, the song took on its final shape. "The premise of the song is that rednecks are everywhere, not just in the Southern United States," Earle himself said. In Kriek's version, justice is done beautifully to the "flesh and blood" of the story. More than an interpretation of the song on paper, Kriek adapts the essence of the song as well.

WHERE THE WILD ROSES GROW is no traditional murder ballad either. Nick Cave did base the song, which he recorded with Kylie Minogue, upon an event which is related in "The Willow Garden," the flipside of his single which was a hit in 1996. A background is explained in neither of the two songs. Why the man kills the Wild Rose with a stone (in "The Willow Gardens" he uses a sabre) is nowhere made clear, except for his threatening opinion that "all beauty must die." In Erik Kriek's version, things happen differently: here the murderer is an escaped convict, Zachary Smalls, who is after the girl's money. She doesn't trust him, and packs a pistol when she goes to the place where the wild roses grow. But in this version, he knocks the gun out of her hand with the stone that is used in the song to kill her. With a sigh of relief, we can verify that she has survived the terrible incident... The coda of the comic is great. "Has anything happened while I was gone?" her mother asks after returning from a visit to the prison where her husband is locked up. "No, nothing ever happens here," Elisa McDay can answer. Not quite truthfully, as we know by then.

CALEB MEYER is a murder ballad written by Gillian Welch, a singer who has many devoted fans among Americana aficionados, and especially those who are attracted by the retro-element that characterizes Welch's repertoire. "Caleb Meyer" can be found on her *Hell Among the Yearlings*, an album steeped in darkness and Biblical references, and "Caleb Meyer" most certainly is not an incongruous item there. Yet, this is not an entirely gloomy song: after all, Caleb Meyer gets what he deserved.

In the Pines is a splendid collection of graphic stories; after reading them I ended up asking for more. If you would accept a broad interpretation of the genre, quite a lot of recent contributions to the Great American Songbook would be fit for graphic adaptation. I would be curious to see Kriek's version of Bob Dylan's "The Lonesome Death of Hattie Carroll" ("William Zanzinger killed poor Hattie Carroll / With a cane that he twirled around his diamond ring finger"), which is based upon a historic event ("this is taken out of the newspapers" Dylan himself said). And what to think of "There Is Something On Your Mind" (originally by Big Jay McNeely, but a hit for Bobby Marchan in 1960) in which the murderer first kills the lover of his adulterous wife, but hesitates to shoot her too. He decides to forgive her, but at that very moment another admirer steps in. And the singer, he can't help himself... "Please baby, I'm sorry, I didn't mean to shoot you..." This genre is what the French call a *mer à boire*. "Hey Joe," "Delia's Gone," "Stagger Lee," "Little Sadie," Lyle Lovett's "L.A. County," "Tom Dooley." Many a song always willing to supply a picture of the darker side of the American Dream... What I mean to say is: America has become hardly less trigger-happy since the era of the Wild West, the years when the first murder ballads were written. Have there been songs written about Jeffrey Dahmer and all those others? There's a lot more work to be done, Erik Kriek!

Erik Kriek (Amsterdam, 1966) is best known in his native Holland for the wordless adventures of faux-superhero Gutsman and his girlfriend Tigra. His 2012 publication *Het Onzienbare (From Beyond)*, a selection of adaptations of stories by H.P Lovecraft, introduced his name to an international audience.

Aside from making comics, Kriek is a prolific illustrator, working for a variety of national and international media, magazines and newspapers. He has also recently started illustrating children's books, taking his work into hitherto uncharted territories.

Erik Kriek lives and works in Amsterdam, the Netherlands, together with his wife Stans and their son, Clovis.

Thank you to Hansje Joustra, Wiebe
Mokken, Jan Donkers, my fellow studio-mates
at Pelikaen Studios, the Blue Grass Boogiemen,
Sophie ter Schure, Annita Langereis, Excelsior
Recordings and my dearest, ever faithful yet
critical proofreader, Stans.

In the Pines is dedicated to my father,
Erik Kriek, Sr. (1931-2013) who, sadly,
only saw the first sketches for this book.

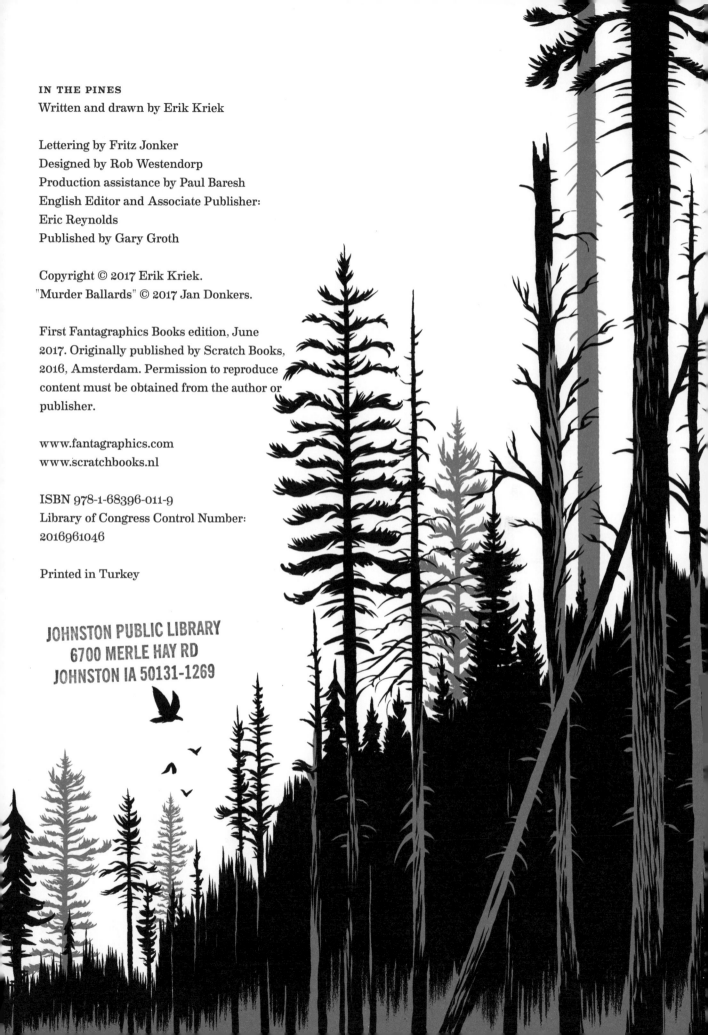

IN THE PINES
Written and drawn by Erik Kriek

Lettering by Fritz Jonker
Designed by Rob Westendorp
Production assistance by Paul Baresh
English Editor and Associate Publisher:
Eric Reynolds
Published by Gary Groth

First Fantagraphics Books edition, June
2017. Originally published by Scratch Books,
2016, Amsterdam. Permission to reproduce
content must be obtained from the author or
publisher.

www.fantagraphics.com
www.scratchbooks.nl

ISBN 978-1-68396-011-9
Library of Congress Control Number:
2016961046

Printed in Turkey